Stewart Henderson

Stewart Henderson was born in Liverpool in 1952, and since his teens has been performing his poetry on radio, television and stage. He has appeared on numerous occasions on BBC Radio's 1, 2, 3, 4 and 5 Live, the World Service, and BBC TV, RTE, ITV as well as various US and European national channels. He has read his work at many major venues throughout the UK, Republic of Ireland, USA and Canada, including London's Royal Albert Hall, Glasgow's SECC, Dublin's National Concert Hall, Belfast's Ulster Hall, Cardiff's St David's Hall, and New York's Lincoln Center for Performing Arts.

Since 1989 Stewart has hosted The Receiving End at The Nave, West London - a series of in-depth interviews before a live audience. His chosen guests have included Michael Heseltine; Tony Benn; Sir Edward Heath; Dr Germaine Greer; Archbishop of York, Dr David Hope; Jeremy Paxman; Anita Roddick; Stephen Fry; John Simpson; Melvyn Bragg; Sir Anthony Dowell; David Montgomery; Lord Archer and the late Paul Eddington.

Stewart is also a published songwriter, and has had commissioned comedy and drama scripts broadcast by, amongst others, S4C, BBC Radio Scotland and Granada TV.

By the same author

Poetry:

CARVED INTO A SCAN
WHOSE IDEA OF FUN IS A NIGHTMARE?
FAN MALE
ASSEMBLED IN BRITAIN
A GIANT'S SCRAPBOOK
HOMELAND

General:

GREENBELT: SINCE THE BEGINNING
ADRIFT IN THE 80S: THE STRAIT INTERVIEWS
(Editor)

STEWART HENDERSON

Limited Edition

Plover Books

First published in 1997
by Plover Books
Redhill Farmhouse
Snitterfield, Stratford upon Avon,
CV37 0PQ

Copyright © Stewart Henderson 1997

The Author asserts the moral right to be
identified as the author of this work

A catalogue record for this book is
available from the British Library

ISBN 0-9530234-0-0

*All rights reserved. No part of this
publication may be reproduced, stored in a
retrieval system, or transmitted, in any form or
by any means without the prior permission of
the publisher. This book is sold subject to the
condition that it shall not, by way of trade or
otherwise, be lent, re-sold, hired out or
otherwise circulated without the publisher's
prior consent in any form of binding or cover
other than that in which it is published and
without a similar condition including this
condition being imposed on the subsequent
purchaser.*

Printed and bound in Great Britain by
Bell and Bain Ltd., Glasgow

For my darling Carol

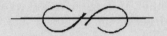

my vital map
through all our
dedicated days

ACKNOWLEDGEMENTS

I-Spy was commissioned by BBC Radio 4; 12 Bar Blues, and Avoiding the Heartbreak of You by BBC Radio Scotland; Don't Miss Christmas, and North Country Cleric by J. John; Let the Vision by the YMCA for their 150th Anniversary; Priestly Duties was written for the Induction Service of Eric Delve; as was Prayer of Aspiration for Carole Parker. Hand of Fellowship was first published in *Third Way;* Everything in Heaven also exists in song form, on the Sony Album *Martyn Joseph,* published by Waif Music.

Other poems were written for various public readings and performances, my thanks to those who organised these events. I wish to convey my immense gratitude to all friends and supporters of *Homeland*, and I reserve an especial mention for John and Jacqui Peet for their encouragement, belief and selfless service in their friendship to us both.

Limited Edition would not exist had it not been for the love, and commitment of Carol - my human hope, my helpmeet, my utter friend, and my wife. She is as much this book as I am.

LIMITED EDITION

TABLE OF CONTENTS

LIMITED EDITION

LUPIN FLOWERS

As soon as the lupin flowers,
it fades;
and it is such a small
spray of a season
where broad bees sup
the mauve wine of foxgloves.

For, when we are young
and casting for life,
we neglect time
leaving it in the cellar
with our swimming certificates
and school-year books.

When older,
we do deals with the past,
imagining ourselves still there,
spring hearted,
ripe as rosemary
and gawky with hope.
Yet where are we in all this time?

From the first flock of freckles,
to the loose curtains
of our winter skin,

where can we stop
and become that which we are?

For now, we will abide,
waiting for time
to do away with itself
so that we can begin again
But this time - timeless -
wild as a buffalo,
pounding with radiance
over marble prairies
and across
rivers of frankincense.

VALENTINE'S DAY

Let love be a gem-cluster chariot
opal and encircling
on and reserved from
the world's pale, pinched streets.

Let love haste straight and far, yet,
not be a race, or test,
but precisely exhibit
the extravagant honours
of care, fellowship and acceptance -
the impossible awards
which the world cannot confer.

Let love take us to the end
and the beginning
of the Heavenly Sea
for us to meet the only craft
shaped like
a cross,
a breached heart
and a bloodstone and bramble crown.

I WANT TO BE

I want to be an elephant
with satellite-dish ears
I want to be a crocodile
and learn to cry real tears

I want to be a silk-worm
and learn the art of sewing
I want to weave beyond the stars
to glimpse where I'll be going

I want to be a blob with horns
that's somehow learned to float
I want to be a tadpole
that turns into a goat

I want to be a yellow song
that snorts across the prairie
I want to be a bison
crossed with a canary

I want to be a soldier ant
in the undergrowth
and if life got too exhausting
I'd desert and be a sloth

I want to be a glamour beast
off on photo-shoots
I want to be a cockatoo
with sulphur-crested roots

I want to be an eider duck
in bobbing, feathered gown.
Does an eider duck without much luck
become quite eider down?

I want to be volcanic
renowned for fiery belches
I want to be a mystery,
something huge that squelches

I want to be a whale
but you'd turn me into soap
I want to be the only lion
to kiss an antelope

I want to be a yucca plant
whose leaves are carefully washed
I want to be fermented grapes
permanently sloshed

I want to be the rainbow trout
no angler ever spliced
I want to be a splinter
in the thumb of Christ

I want to be the rising sun
that never goes to bed
And I wonder what I'll be
when nature rises from the dead?

LIMITED EDITION

On warm highlands
made of arches and meadows
a celebration is taking place
so much is going on

Carefully arranged flowers
are asking a snow leopard
to teach them to roar;
a chuckling bee is astonishing
a spider
by using its web as a trampoline
whilst a pegasus
has settled on the pollen morning
his ivory mane now
a new light year.
As the universe begins to sing
a mud-mosaic hippopotamus
rolls in a gold-leaf lagoon,
some giant sequoias
impressed by the metabolism of
the mouse
have stooped to count
her quill whiskers
and a flock of pebbles
float off
smitten by the clouds' wanderings

And, into all this pageant
this unsettling, unshakeable
paradise
where rivers ascend
and mountains flow,
comes
you, and only you
you, the unique
you man
you woman
you, the limited edition,
you, the no other,
holding an invitation
embossed with coral
and lion's breath

as hovering crowns of
humming birds
lead the applause.

THIS BIG GOD

This big God,
with the sun stroked
by his blue-sky fingers,
bush-burning orb bearing down
on this slight planet
where twigs and eider duck
hold the holiness more than the
high-trumpet coronations
of earth's rickety thrones.

This immense God
rides bareback bold
through the lacquer nights
churning up deep divots of stars
the sparkling soil of heaven's gallops
where the hurdles
reach out past space
and his horse
snorts and steams solemn incense.

This intangible God
bubble blowing his colours
on to creeping things,
growling things, squeaking things,
waving things.

This very much God
full of vast and quantum tricks.

This big, broad God,
child-like,
and storm brooding,
so beyond us
as we linger here,
pining,
brittle,
in His Name.

CHECK-OUT GIRL

I'm a check-out girl
I'm a check-out girl
I'm a check-out girl
I'm a check-out girl

I didn't do no good at school
got no GCSE's
what's the point of trying
when you've got no-one to please
so I got this job shelf-filling
where low pay is the norm
and then I got presented with
this shapeless uniform
We're not la-de-da like Waitrose
or posh like M & S
we're more like Happy Shopper
without the happiness

I'm a check-out girl
I'm a check-out girl
and I let him take a peck
I'm a check-out girl
I'm a check-out girl
with love-bites round me neck

I got an interview for Sainsbury's
I hate their orange bags
and they asked what I thought
hummus was,
I said: 'A Greek man cracking gags'
I wear this stained-cravat-like thing
I like to think it's silk
and that I'm dead sophisticated
like a box of Liebfraumilch

I'm a check-out girl
I'm a check-out girl
and I let him take a peck
I'm a check-out girl
I'm a check-out girl
with love-bites round me neck
I'm a check-out girl
I'm a check-out girl
and he took me on a date
I'm a check-out girl
I'm a no-hope girl
now me period is late
now me period is late
'cos me period's so late.

LET THE VISION

Born out of a different age,
held on history's flaking page
the gleam of Empire's polished boots
the Workhouse, rickets,
slave trade routes;
the wheezing waif
with soot-lined chest
rammed into the chimney breast.
Within the huddles of the weak,
a prayer of dreams begins to speak.

Let the vision be a vision,
and a vision yet to come;
a community of healing
for the shrivelled and the numb
where the golden river ripples
and the Cross becomes a jewel
above the Throne of contradictions
where the beaten get to rule.

Now we dwell in other days
chained to our consumer ways
through mantras of
'Acquire', and 'Keep',
whilst single parent families sleep
outside the city's neon doors,

as we pursue the Pilgrim's cause -
our earnest wish to liberate
and help the meek participate.

Let the vision be a vision,
and a vision yet to come;
a community of healing
for the shrivelled and the numb
where the golden river ripples
and the Cross becomes a jewel
above the Throne of contradictions
where the beaten get to rule.

Kingdoms of the strong will rise
and burn the sayings of the wise
while power fills its vaults with dust
and steal the frail rags of the just;
we'll serve the Saviour of the low
who soothes those in arrears to woe.
Our Man of Sorrows, broken gem,
the mercy found at Bethlehem

Let the vision be a vision,
and a vision yet to come;
a community of healing
for the shrivelled and the numb
where the golden river ripples
and the Cross becomes a jewel
above the Throne of contradictions
where the beaten get to rule.

CROWN SUSPECT

He must have been wicked
Did he break any laws?
Did he steal cash from widows,
or humiliate whores?

Why is he up there?
Did he do perverse things?
But what do you expect
from penniless kings?

The gouging of kindness
His scraping of breath
The closing of heaven
The prowling of death

The ripping of sinew
His heart leaking out
The melting of goodness
His ambivalent shout

His body unpinioned
The burial grounds
The wailing of wombs,
and, the whining of hounds

The fragrant entombing
His vinegar lips
The desolate clouds
The charcoal eclipse

Subversive servant
Speechless Messiah
Priest of the ruined
Chariot of fire

He must have been wicked
Did he break any laws?
Did he steal cash from widows,
or humiliate whores?

Why is he up there?
Did he do perverse things?
But what do you expect
from penniless kings?

17

PRIESTLY DUTIES
written for E.D. - 23.5.96.

What should a priest be?
All things to all -
male, female and genderless
What should a priest be?
reverent and relaxed
vibrant in youth
assured through the middle years
divine sage when ageing

What should a priest be?
accessible and incorruptible
abstemious, yet full of celebration,
informed, but not threateningly so,
and far above
the passing soufflé of fashion

What should a priest be?
an authority on singleness
Solomon-like on the labyrinth
of human sexuality
excellent with young marrieds,
old marrieds, were marrieds, never
marrieds, shouldn't have marrieds,
those who live together, whose who live
apart, and those
who don't live anywhere

respectfully mindful of senior
citizens and war veterans,
familiar with the ravages of arthritis
osteoporosis, post-natal depression,
anorexia, whooping-cough and nits.

What should a priest be?
all-round family person
counsellor, but not officially because
of the recent changes in legislation,
teacher, expositor, confessor,
entertainer, juggler,
good with children, and
possibly sea-lions,
empathetic towards pressure groups

What should a priest be?
on nodding terms with
Freud, Jung, St John of The Cross,
The Scott Report, The Rave Culture,
The Internet, the Lottery, BSE, and
Anthea Turner,
pre-modern, fairly modern,
post-modern, and, ideally,
secondary-modern -
if called to the inner city

What should a priest be?
charismatic, if needs must,
but quietly so,
evangelical, and thoroughly
meditative, mystical, but not
New Age.
Liberal, and so open to other voices,
traditionalist, reformer and
revolutionary
and hopefully, not on medication
unless for an old sporting injury.

Note to congregations:

If your priest actually fulfills all of the
above, and then enters the pulpit one
Sunday morning wearing nothing but a
shower-cap, a fez, and declares: 'I'm the
King and Queen of Venus, and we shall
now sing the next hymn in Latvian,
take your partners, please'. -
Let it pass.
Like you and I,
they too sew the thin thread of humanity.
Remember Jesus in the Garden -
beside himself?

So, what does a priest do?
mostly stays awake
at Deanery synods
tries not to annoy the Bishop
too much
visits hospices, administers comfort,
conducts weddings, christenings, -
not necessarily in that order,
takes funerals
consecrates the elderly to the grave
buries children, and babies,
feels completely helpless beside
the swaying family of a suicide.

What does a priest do?
tries to colour in God
uses words to explain miracles
which is like teaching
a millipede to sing, but
even more difficult.

What does a priest do?
answers the 'phone
when sometimes they'd rather not
occasionally errs and strays
into tabloid titillation,

prays for Her Majesty's Government

What does a priest do?
tends the flock through time,
oil and incense,
would secretly like each PCC
to commence
with a mud-pie making contest
sometimes falls asleep when praying
yearns, like us, for
heart-rushing deliverance

What does a priest do?
has rows with their family
wants to inhale Heaven
stares at bluebells
attempts to convey the mad love of God
would like to ice-skate with crocodiles
and hear the roses when they pray.

How should a priest live?

How should we live?

As priests,
transformed by The Priest

that death prised open
so that he could be our priest
martyred, diaphanous and
matchless priest.

What should a priest be?

What should a priest do?

How should a priest live?

A NORTH COUNTRY CLERIC
talks to God about his calling,
20 years later

When I was first commissioned
and crammed with student flash
full of hermeneutics
with compulsory shaving rash

Who'd have thought that I would grow
into such maturity
as I earnestly ask God
'Could you slay the PCC?'

My ministry's been adapted
from Apostolic zeal -
to sitting, drawing badly
a Barometer Appeal

I christen and I bury
without the Psalmist's lyre
yet beside the grave's privation
let me howl, and then inspire

through Ezekiel's astral pictures
and Daniel's placid lions -
meanwhile, my weak fire's choking
with far too many irons

And Wigan isn't Patmos
where visions leave me stunned;
Did Jesus really send me out
to boost the Fabric Fund?

On TV we're Trollope's schemers
jockeying for Dean,
whilst this member of Melchizedek
writes the parish magazine

Though we've conferences and
                              seminars
and workshops on Belief
we've children dead in swing-parks
and bewildered, sound-bite grief

Our Zeitgeist's 'plausibility',
and it's 'wise' PR to sell
a jumper-wearing, chatty God
shamed by the creed of Hell

So now, God of youth and ageing
as the Faith roams thro' this maze
Make me Priest and a Preserver
in this Wilderness of Days.

LIVERPOOL MEDITATION

Is this the land of milk and honey?
The one for which this city gave,
conscripted youth to War's dark waters,
Woodbine battalions of the brave.
This city of abandoned vehicles,
bankrupt stock and playtime crack.
Promised land of little promise,
a gaunt, consumer, cul-de-sac.

When we were young, Orwell, Priestley,
chastened us with postcards home
writing of a TB Kingdom,
a cloth-capped land of monochrome.
And as for their HP descendants,
cocooned in space with Satellite,
not knowing of the word, redemption,
owned by the loan-shark's knock at
                              night

Is this the land of milk and honey
where birdsong seldom cleans the air?
And all around is glass confetti
and only strangers pause to stare.
Absorbed into the locals' spirits,
demons of despondency,

souls and bodies soaked in debt,
crying out for Jubilee.

Yet Heaven lingers in these side-
                          streets,
amidst the metal-shutter shops,
where lethal games played with
                          syringes
have long replaced kids' spinning
                          tops.
And Heaven lodges in these side-
                          streets
feeling each tormenting pain
swallowing each tranquilliser
visiting the barely sane.

This is a land of milk and honey,
and perpetual alarms,
full of light and sawn-off menace,
a daily paradox of psalms.
This is a land of milk and honey,
bereft of bud and bursting leaves,
though glory may not seem apparent
- a place where Goodness lives and
                          breathes.

MY INTENTION

It was ever my intention
to speak to you this way -
not through the vexed sword
of the gouging snow-wind,
but from the tethered throat
of my low-lying lamb,
my thicket-jailed sacrosanct.

It was ever my intention
to let loose the meek this way -
not with blaring parades
of thin-ice certainty,
but through the vandalised heart
of my hanging child,
my grated-flesh go-between,
my thorn-padlocked scapegoat,
my ruined original.

It was ever my intention
to show you Me this way -
through the modest and vulnerable
who are my unexpected symbol,
my contradictory sign -
the intoxicating wafer,
the coherent wine.

It was ever my intention
for you
to wear the crown
of paradox
being aware of the gathering hunt
but ready
to rule and reign
from foxes' holes.

HAND OF FELLOWSHIP

You walk too free for us
for we are dying here, comfortably,
and in control

What we fear in you, is that
you are too tender for the game;
we did not start out this way,
we were once rosy in warm shawls
but on our way
to becoming immaculate
we realised that everything
has to be in its place,
and that's why we put you in yours.

We do not like the way you gasp
at the rhododendron's fire,
or your cherishing
of useless animals;
it attracts too many of the gullible

We've even begun to copy you
as a means of reducing your effect;
it doesn't sound the same when
we say it,
but our salons are crammed with
everyone, bar the wise

Still, we've contained you,
and not even your slight song
from out beyond the marshes
will rattle the perfumed locks
of our counterfeit kingdom.

Some of us really do want to know
your secret
but we can't break ranks, you see,
it's not encouraged.
Being right has its drawbacks,
it's the cross we have to bear.

AND WHAT IF . . .

*'In vain do romantic lovers of poetry
think that if governments were run
not by politicians but by poets, there
would be paradise. I fear that the
world could find itself daily in a state
of war.'*

Yevgeny Yevtushenko

And what if governments
were run by poets?

Would legislation rhyme
and statutes read as sonnets
would finance bills speculate
'what is wealth compared to a
million butterflies?'
Would filing cabinets stand empty,
helter-skeltered by perfumed
starfish of clematis,
if governments were run by poets?

And what if governments
were run by poets?

Would their opponents use cliché
and posture to discredit them -

miming the drinking of laudanum
during the debates, and going on
to feign consumption, poverty,
idleness and deviancy?

And what if governments
were run by poets?

Would luminous vested road workers
have to spend a mandatory hour
every day
looking for God
whilst imagining themselves
eternal mountains yet unclambered?

And how would governments,
run by poets,
approach the roulette wheel
of history . . . ?
Because peace is good for poets,
for that's when they write of
the gathering apocalypse
And, if all then collapses,
the bewildered streets full of braying,
would citizens be ordered,
at gun-point,

to be still and consider
the texture of a tulip
by a government run by poets?

And what if governments
were run by poets?

Would they seek
to exterminate
other poets -
distrustful of their motives,
their standing,
and their reviews,
envious of their advances?
Would death squads be formed,
land mines sold,
and torture agreed upon,
as the ruling poets of the day
fingered lace,
listened to Haydn,
smearing their lips with port?

Beware a government run by poets
because they hear your thoughts
they study your feelings.

Poets stand
outside
halls of mirrors,
contemplating the soul's deformities,
and asking the blackbird,
why does it still sing?

Beware a government run by poets.

OTHER PEOPLE

Other people are tourists
with their airport thrillers,
caravans and semolina skin

Other people are greedy
with their duty-free day trips,
hotel carveries and bloated weekends

Other people are annoying
with their woodchipped flower beds,
bookless shelves and
dithering in banks

Other people are voiceless
with their sparse 'fridges,
blank beds and tuneless humming

Other people are unremarkable
other people are other people
I'm not like other people

AVOIDING THE HEARTBREAK
OF YOU

We stand before these witnesses
here present
and state our vows
although state is far too
dogmatic a word -
as we now suggest to one another
the following deliberations for bliss:
Sex will be, at all times, negotiated
and never spontaneous
as that could lead to lack of control,
emotional domination,
or, worse still, selfish gratification.
We will operate a policy of
non-tactile, militant consideration
and complete a memo with little
flowers on it
when requesting consent
to touch one another;
and, unless agreed beforehand,
we will never, ever, invade
each other's space -
be it physical, or parking.
We will hold compatible views
so as not to cause embarrassment
amongst acquaintances,
or give the impression of

division between us.
Prospective friends will be interviewed
at neutral locations,
and, over dinner, invited
to fill in our questionnaire -
canvassing their opinions on
politics, religion and interior design.
We will avidly read an agreed-upon
selection of lifestyle magazines,
and meaningful novels.
We will develop our own
internal ambience
for the greater good of the community
We will abhor all 'isms'
and anything which could be
considered quirky.
We will prepare all
our meals together,
harmonising on a menu beforehand.
In this way, we will have created joy,
legislated happiness.
Should either of us feel the need
to be humorous with each other
then the content of such expression
should not cause offence,
be completely intelligible to all

sections of society,
and avoid any reference to bottoms.
We will not drink to excess
as we will be complete.
We will sit, squat, meditate
and recline,
on only natural products.
We will not have pets,
as that is irresponsible,
and robs nature of its different voice.
We will not smoke.
We will drive unleaded.
We will refrain from all team games,
and any activity where
competition is encouraged.
We will have no rough edges
and, should resentment arise
in either party, for whatever reason,
we will unpack it, search our respective
psyches, and, if no solution can be
found, we will walk into the forest
naked, and wail
at the spirits of our ancestors.
So now, in closing,
let us say, together 'I Love You'
provisionally.

12 BAR BLUES

The first bar was quite empty
I claimed a thigh high stool
ordered some nostalgia
and thought of Liverpool

In the second I turned maudlin
as Celts are prone to do,
had a sentimental wallow
as I chewed the burnt black brew

By the third the muse was stirring,
went into writing mode
Desert Orchid, Trigger, Shergar,
a poem in horse code

In the fourth I started glowing
and had enormous thoughts
that were published via a contract
which advanced me lots of noughts

In the fifth I got quite chatty
and oozed a love of life
told a joke about a funeral
to a man who'd lost his wife

In the sixth, my eye now swelling,
I joined a leaving do,
shed tears with Kim from Planning
who's been transferred to Crewe

At the seventh, speech is floppy
I stand and sway a bit
a gorilla buys me shorts
but they don't quite seem to fit

The eighth is blurred and blaring
a Thrash band beat the walls
In the Gents urinals flush fast,
a glazed Niagara Falls

The ninth, tenth and eleventh
are a mystery that won't rest,
I'm not sure how they happened
an erased Marie Celeste

By the twelfth I can remember
Regrets I've had a few
caused by the lips of drink
after arguments with you.

BIRTHDAY CARD

I used to love my mother
then she had to go away
I tried to love my father
although he went the same way
I took my love to school
where someone called me fat
Now I'm trying to love myself
but I'm not too good at that.

NEW MOVES

The bedroom is looking
quite decent
though there isn't much room
for my books
and I've yet to invent a home for
my collection of porcelain ducks

The telephone man comes
tomorrow
think I'll cheer myself up
with some flowers
I'm afraid I'll mix up my
new number
with the one that used to be ours.

WAGTAIL

This summer eve
in Scotland's swathes
the burn leaps long
from the green belly of the hills,
and the sun lilts low
in the sapling sky.

Above the gleeful water
in the shallow, stone wall,
nests a secret;
a new, Dead Sea Scrolls
too delicate to breathe near.
An ancient truth a few hours old.
A pied wagtail arrows out
in front of us,
leaving a frail cradle of
dried grasses and seed-size hearts.

The occupants,
a précis of nature's pilgrimage:
two unhatched eggs,
cloister-quiet and membrane-caped;
behind them, a couple of chicks,
their orange threaded beaks
open and waving
as if gulping for heaven.

Whilst, to their side,
prostrate and bow-legged,
a sprawled casualty
of something we can't know;
comic and dignified,
a premature fossil.

This a momentary glimpse
at a fortune,
as we peered intensely
before speeding away -
longing for the parent
to return
to its uncoordinated inheritance.

LINDISFARNE PRIORY,
SUMMER EVENING

For now,
God is still with himself
and he smells old and wise
and full of grief,
as the brilliant windows
with too many stories
illustrate this moment.

Outside, a curlew
ripples her throat
like a waterfall;
singing, as she always has,
gathering songs of baptism.

Lines of Humble Advice Addressed to the Poet, Burns, on the Announcement of his Return

Welcome back to Scotland, Rabbie,
it's network nirvana,
whirlpool celebrity
from now on, Rabbie.
It's wall to wall meetings, and
personal appearances.
So here's your itinerary,
your mobile 'phone,
your pin number, your cash card,
some useful e-mail addresses,
names of a tax consultant,
therapist,
important professional types, and,
knowing how doomy
you poets can get,
contact details for an Exit counsellor.

So choose life, Rabbie,
choose mortgage payments,
choose washing machines,
choose the Mel Gibson Fish Farm
Share Option,
choose Begbie as the
new Ronald McDonald.

Choose Easterhouse, or
Wester Hailes, Rabbie.
Choose Bearsden, or Cumbernauld.
Choose Highland, Lowland,
choose Shetland in summer
when the Norse gods have
smoothed the cream beaches.
Welcome back to Scotland, Rabbie.

I don't want to sorrow you, Rabbie,
but since you left,
you've ended up cute,
embossed on shortbread tins
in tartan shops in Moffat -
which I suppose is no more
bizarre than
Bob Dylan-shaped hash cakes
in Amsterdam cafes.

Being a national figure
of some distinction, Rabbie,
you've already received invitations
to attend
Masonic suppers,
SNP Press Conferences,
Caledonian Balls,

Ceilidhs,
Settler Watch evenings,
the Braemar Games,
Celtic Connections,
dinner at Balmoral,
both pro and anti field sports'
associations, and,
there are also several
unpleasant letters from
the Child Support Agency.

And then, Rabbie, you'll be giving
public readings at Waterstone's,
several Central Belt Rave Clubs,
literary festivals, Runrig gigs,
Iona Abbey, the Mayfest,
and the
Official and Fringe Festivals.

And, all the while, Rabbie,
you'll be trying to work out -
Where is Scotland?
Which is Scotland?
What is Scotland?

Leisure Scotland,

Investment Scotland,
Film Star Scotland,
Gaelic Scotland,
Grieving Scotland,
Corgi Scotland,
McAllister's penalty against England
Scotland,
Flower of Scotland,
Clearance Scotland,
Rab C Hamish Macbeth 12th July
Scotland,
Scotland the Brave,
Scotland the Slave,
Scotland the Caged,
Scotland Enraged.

The Union continues to be
a barbed-wire handshake, Rabbie,
and you've been invited on to an
STV 'phone-in -
live yelling debate from the
Kelvin Hall (which station
executives are hoping will be
rowdier than the preferred
Usher Hall, and hence,
better television).

You'll be on a panel alongside
a Bishop, a Cardinal, a Moderator,
some MPs, several London-based
lairds and, inevitably, Andrew Neil.

And when asked your views, Rabbie,
you will plead with us to consider
the displaced mouse,
the wounded hare,
the view from the plough,
the half-death that is poverty,
the consuming storms of the flesh,
the liberation that is love,
the noose that tightens when we
sing with the Devil,
the beguiling stench of all piety,
and
the lice on all our bonnets.

This, Rabbie, will be very
laudable - Sir Harry Laudable -
see, that's what you'll need to
cultivate, Rabbie - smart,
flip, sound-bites.

You see, Rabbie, your spontaneous

language of the heart
could well cause an
uncomfortable silence
which will have to be covered
by a sponsored ad-break
made by the Tourist Board,
featuring a vista of sepia lochs,
muscular, bearded swankies,
and unblemished, red-haired bonnies
And, Rabbie, you will feel
confused, and will be
shunned in Hospitality afterwards.

And you will conclude that
perhaps Scotland,
like heaven,
is so much
and so many
and so big
somewhere else -
too vast to consider,
too sacred to describe,
fleetingly visible only in the
incense mists,
and faintly explained by
the gargling grouse,

and the bubble-throat-balladeer curlew
and the piped battlefield battalions
of the innumerable ghosts of the slain
wandering unseen past
the air-brake tourist coaches.

So, Rabbie, as you, all alone,
melancholy up Byres Road
what will you be thinking?

Tell us what to think -
these are days of
so many opinions, Rabbie,
but few voices
and inadequate visions.

Tell us, Rabbie,
was Steinbeck right?
Must Scotland remain
the unwon cause?

Tell us, Rabbie, tell us.
    'Go on, sweet bird,
    and soothe our care,
    Thy tuneful notes
    will hush despair.'

STARS

We do not look at the stars anymore
and, if we do,
we do not know what they mean
or even
why they stare at us
the silver gaze of the
Universe's deep eyes following
us home
As for what's behind them
we can only speculate
Forests yet to come
and the waste of all our wars
innumerable
heavy-headed mammoths
and babies that were finished with
Why do we sleep
when there's all this to consider?
We should stay up
and listen to the galaxies sighing
and plot our journey
that is to come
when we will go far beyond
the small spaces of these days -
out, into the unseen,
floating tundra of Paradise,
or Elsewhere.

NIGHT WATCH AT LEWISHAM HOSPITAL

For two nights
I watched you fumbling
through unconsciousness,
and although I had no camera
my eyes possess the negatives:
images of tubes
and get-well cards,
weeping flowers
and your face
lyrical with truth
as pain launched its offensive.
O my amourette!
to see your closed eyes
flickering, though flameless,
temporarily hidden
by the twilight of anguish.
You are now
where I have never been
as I send my meagre love
through
the opaque entrance of suffering.

HAVING LOOKED

Having looked at the earth,
scowling with clouds,
the Constellations began fleeing -
luminous refugees
gathering about them
their bright babies.

History has discoloured
the exact moment of exile
but older, bearded meteors remember
the bursting Apple as
Cain's first weapon.
After that came the
cacophonous bombs
which infant particles,
innocent of the impious heart,
mistook as thunderstorms
and God amusing himself.

Others, having grown heavenly
on the blinding milk
of their mother's radiant breasts,
know the savage legends to be true;
they have seen
their first rocket
watched the slow, bacterial

blink of satellites,
glanced down and heard
the rivers ill with themselves

And, like their sparkling ancestors,
the Constellations continue
to hasten away from
the rogue Empire of earth,
distrustful of any promises it makes
through its coarse calculations
and asthmatic speeches.

Yet still,
the astral armadas outwith the skies
sail onward,
the seeping scent of another land
steering them home.

PRAYER OF ASPIRATION
Written for C.P. - 18.12.96.

This is my heart -
my full heart;
brimming and hungry to serve you
deserve you
through life's banquets and wakes
and our ordinary afternoons
where nothing is apparent
apart from the sky's subtle palette
and the sound of
our children's skin, growing.

This is my life,
my small life,
humbled and being made better
by the passionate Lamb;
eager to be here with you
and share with you
the radiant landscapes
of our near and deep God.

This is my aim,
my honourable aim,
to refuse the robes of domination,
but to put on
the vestments of compassion,
to form in you,

and for you to form in me,
the dignity of God
the pattern of Jesus
and the kindness of the Holy Spirit
for the benefit of us all -
our church, our community,
and our world -
and for the eminence
of the Lord of all.

All in the Name of our
slandered Saviour,
acquitted Messiah,
and returning
Beloved Bridegroom and King.
                              Amen

THE LAND THAT BREAKS
BEYOND OUR DREAMS

The land that breaks
beyond our dreams
has crocuses that do not dip
below the earth of winter;
and it is only their mood there
which makes the petals cup in prayer
or spread with joy

The land that breaks
beyond our dreams
only breathes the virgin air
of itself, and the roaming rainbows
of its ribbon afternoons;
when the birdsong scoops the
too-long dead from our
mean, untidy graves.

The land that breaks
beyond our dreams
is where the drained begin to leap
and the faint rustle of the
butterfly's waltz
is enough to kneel you deep,
tame with yourself
and sluiced of all your woes.

The land that breaks
beyond our dreams
where all that glory comes beside us,
and surging shoals of daffodils
surf across an ocean, or,
perhaps a cloud;
that will be when
there is no more proud;
and the missing, the mad,
and the cowed,
will know how to sing descant
with the voice behind the nightingale.

I-SPY

I spied 50's Liverpool
I spied Anfield Road
I spied modest rose-beds
my father finely hoed
I spied the Carlton Cinema
and films of love and war
I spied Terry Thomas
driving a Morgan Plus 4

I spied our first television
in a shop without alarms
I spied my Sunday School Teacher
wearing lucky charms
I spied black and white farces
starring Brian Rix
I spied Pele at Goodison Park in 1966

I spied the mountains of Lebanon
beneath a twilight claret sky
I spied the Dakota
Imagine . . . having to die
I spied the jungles of Thailand
with mosquitoes the size of a mouse
I spied the Beverly Sisters
in the foyer of Broadcasting House

There are lots of things
I've never spied
such as cheerleaders who frown
a politician lost for words
a rainbow upside down
a grounded angel with vertigo
the end of all despair
And I've never met Big Chief I-Spy
I'm not sure he's even there.

TROUBLED EVENSONG

We find God so embarrassing
we seed of English earth
but we will swell and rally to
preserve the Virgin Birth
From ancient lineage we hail
and withering estates
where foreigners shoot grouse
because we have to pay the rates

We find God too uncomfortable
to claim Him as our own
we do not wish to listen to
Golgotha's ravaged moan
Yet watch us throttle bishops
who have their liberal say
so we can stand in silent prayer
upon Remembrance Day

We find God too inscrutable
which suits us rather well
so conserve selective breeding
and send the rest to Hell
For that is where we've come from
though others call it school
the cane of deprivation
for all those sired to rule

We find God so embarrassing
but when Kings College Choir
sing Stainer's stirring Anthem
we look to matters higher
And 'though death will leave us naked
there's something else far worse
we'll have to seek forgiveness
when we rise from the hearse.

INSTANT FABLE

I knew a man called Instant
who lived an instant creed
he sought an instant lifestyle
to suit his instant need

He purchased matt, black gimmicks
and gadgets without cords
and all he prized were instant
consumerist rewards

He scanned the instant papers
their instant views of life
he went computer dating
and met an instant wife

Throughout the global village
he took some instant trips
became a culture expert
through learning instant tips

He bought an instant camera
for instant memories
no time for contemplation
as that may stir unease

And all he loved was instant
no thoughts for the unseen
with instant entertainment
upon his instant screen

He passed a motor showroom
in which a car gleamed bright
he bought it in an instant
and drove it home that night

He sped an instant journey
too fast for one sharp bend
he hit some Cable roadworks
and met an instant end.

THE COLLECTIVE LUNG OF
LIT AND LANG

In the English Common Room
the kettle doesn't work
well, it would if somebody fixed it
but that's a job for more
practical types -
chemists, mathematicians,
woodworkers made of custard
gabbling goblins with screwdrivers
ambidextrous sea-serpents -
that's the thing about
teaching English
you can feel useless but
be imaginative at the same time.

It's beyond us all this science
we haven't touched the kettle
since it passed on
because we thought if you
dropped glowing elements
into water
you could electrocute someone -
like throwing a two-bar fire
into the bath,
a sort of DIY Jacuzzi
for incompetents.

But then, how do
submarines glow and bleep
in the dark, silver depths
without frying the occupants?
Science, it's beyond us,
and, beyond us
India, water-melons, the Moon.
There we go, being fanciful again.

The thing about English is
you get to teach sprawling
fifteen year olds
(bubbling with blackheads and
hormones)
17th Century metaphysical
love poetry.
Our visionary government
education advisors
certainly know a thing or two
about modern youth -
swarms of enquiring adolescents
skateboarding
while quoting John Donne;
happy infants, lolly-ice sticks
in the spokes of their bikes
arguing knowledgeably about Keats.

That's the thing about
teaching English
you rely on irony -
irony is disappointment
wearing a corset.

See what words can do children.
No, you can't go to the toilet,
it's nearly time for the bell.
A corset, Damian, is an object
which restricts - like a syllabus.

Education teaches you things
makes you practical.
We'll all soon be a nation
of mechanics with nothing to do
but acquire, collect and
tidy away that which makes us
ask, why?

Why a water buffalo?
Why sun spots and withered flowers?

Science and English -
the poetry of the Elements,
        they don't have to be exclusive.

In the right hands
education is dynamite.

Is that why
it's being taken from us?

Chairs on tables, children,
and don't forget,
education
is a wonderful thing.

KEATS'S OTHER LAST WORDS
(After visiting Keats' house in Rome)

All letters written,
and this one:

Italy will be gold
with, or without, me;
babbling place
gilded with hills,
where I am to be no more.

Thrush sings that fellow,
more than my wet lungs.

There is a small fire
in the grate
yet how does it burn
compared to God?

All I am, a poet -
disappointed before the grave,
beyond which
the quieting of this frail stomach
and then,
the finding of my blazing soul.

SECOND POST

I was going to write you a poem
about something wizened and wise
which had waterfalls, angels
and lightning
and a chart of invisible skies

I was going to 'phone, but discreetly
ask the nurse if you'd had
a good night
I thought best
not to bother your family
Not one will be feeling too bright

And why does grief's
fever sweat clichés and
make us so lyrically poor?
I should spew up
volcanoes of feelings;
a life that once was, is no more.

I was hoping to come up and see you
but instead I got out my black tie
and I've written a poem that's
pointless
all it says is 'I hope you don't die'.

ASHES TO ASHES

And where did he go?
and where did he go?
and what is it like?
and what has he seen?
a shapeless adventure
through other world mists?
what shines beyond
mortality's screen?

And why did he go?
and why did he go?
and what switched him off?
and what took him where?
a shocking extraction of
breath from his bones?
and who took him up
Valhalla's stair?

And now that he's gone
and now that he's gone
and what do we say?
and what should we think?
gamble with God on
threescore and ten
knowing each step
is nearer the brink?

THE SPACE BETWEEN US

The space between us is enormous
you breathed fire before the aeon
lit our nights with sprinkled neon
yet we return a mumbled paean
the space between us is enormous

The space between us is tremendous
we speculate how we were hewn
explore mosaics of the moon
and drown your omnipresent tune
the space between us is tremendous

The space between us is prodigious
as we decode the gamma ray,
and comets graze the Milky Way,
an otter dips below the day
the space between us is prodigious

The space between us is enormous
you who speak the celestial tongue
composed the elements of dung
then joined us on the bottom rung
so there may not be
this space   between us.

LISTEN!

When every moon has passed
and the earth's servant grass
is done with all grazing
we will listen

When starfish and magnolias
open their veins to sing
and other, unknown worlds join in
we will listen

When butterflies settle on us
and creatures we can't name
but smell of sapphires,
weave about and between,
we will listen

Yet, before this broad ecstasy,
when the Judge and Lover
of this drizzling world, now
heaves his abattoir cross
through our ironed and folded lives,
do we listen?

When the broken, and the barren,
and the shedding,
beg the wind to deliver them

and the dusk to cleanse
their breath,
do we listen?

When the beyond-us God
of crucifix, crypt and crown
strikes Himself dumb
to get us to hear,
do we listen?

When the smallest of us,
the slightest of us,
the lamb, or lion-like of us,
speak -
do we listen?

Listen!
Listen!
Listen!
In the courts of the outcasts,
Wisdom is giving counsel.

HAVING THE HEART

The documentary camera pans
past empty feeding bowls
As I sit here with plenty
yet famine in my soul
Huddled on this sofa,
my toes snug in deep pile
A matching curtain's victim
who's overdosed on style.

Embarrassed by conviction,
I channel hop in haste
Weary with possessions,
I contemplate the waste
of emaciated infants
expiring through abuse
I don't want to feel this guilty
I just want to be of use

Christ the tiger, Christ the lion,
Christ the one who prowls
Rage of Heaven - I've gone deaf
I cannot hear your growls -
Nourish me with passion
regardless of the cost
Betroth me to the helpless
through your Love Song for the lost.

REMAINDERS OF THE DAY

Books written
Contracts signed
Critics expound
Sometimes unkind

Celebrity signings
Promotional drive
Very few words
actually survive.

DON'T MISS CHRISTMAS

Don't miss Christmas
whilst yearning for the snow
and planning deft manoeuvres
towards the mistletoe
The turkey turning golden
as the sprouts begin to steam
the pudding glazed with brandy
and smashed on double cream

Don't miss Christmas
as mince pies singe your tongue
and you scowl behind your port
at decorations badly hung
where strange relations gather
like a loud, annoying swarm
when the fat logs spit and crackle,
but the homeless can't keep warm

Don't miss Christmas
beware the muddled shelves
displaying Game Boy reindeer
destroying Santa's elves
whilst Mortal Kombat shepherds
chase dragons through the town
the three kings never showed
their helicopter's been shot down

Don't miss Christmas
absorb the silent night
and watch the mucous Saviour
arrive from heaven's height
as in the holy darkness
a virgin strains, then cries,
God's helpless, breathing icon
appears with Mary's sighs

Don't miss Christmas -
the magic of it all
our brittle, gift-wrapped anthem
sleeps in a cattle stall
as the poor and lost and starving
weakly start to sing
it seems only desperate subjects
recognise their King.

EVERYTHING IN HEAVEN

Everything in heaven comes apart:
the atom and the tsetse fly,
deceits which we now justify,
the zebra's stripe, the callous joke,
the anthem that the bullfrogs croak,
the nightingale, the damning phrase,
the unseen rage of all our days,
the beetle's brain, the sour jibe,
the self-advancement moral bribe;
the leper's soul, the withered heart,
everything in heaven comes apart.

Comes apart, explains itself
and shows its complex ways
to see at last is to be free
from our complicated maze
and everything that's chained
will come apart.

Everything in heaven comes apart:
the tuning fork, the afternoon,
the anxious scowl of each baboon;
the bottle brush, the swing top bin,
the lumps that grow beneath our skin
the roulette wheel, conspiring talk,

the rhythm of the penguin's walk,
the years of grief, the libellous hint,
the plasma of the innocent;
the untraced lie, the verbal dart;
everything in heaven comes apart.

Comes apart, explains itself
and shows its complex ways
to see at last is to be free
from our complicated maze
and everything that's chained
will come apart.

Everything in heaven comes apart:
the pogo stick, the monkey gland,
the bloody strife fought overland;
the private scam, the public face,
the press release attempt at grace,
the olive branch, the passport queue,
the 15-minute super loo,
the parrot's blink, the gamma ray,
the things the dead would like to say,
the daffodil, the words that smart
everything in heaven comes apart.

Comes apart, explains itself
and shows its complex ways
to see at last is to be free
from our complicated maze
and everything that's chained
will come apart.

Everything in heaven comes apart:
the diamond ring, the ocean's song,
the conversation that went wrong,
the dry stone wall, the forest fire,
the smile that turned into desire,
the rising sun, the chain-store suit,
the blank gaze of the destitute;
the tender kiss, the pious mask,
the questions that we meant to ask,
the plans we had but couldn't start,
everything in heaven comes apart.

Comes apart, explains itself
and shows its complex ways
to see at last is to be free
from our complicated maze;

and everything that's chained
will come apart
and everything that's locked
will come apart
and everything that's bound
will come apart
for
everything, in Heaven,
comes apart . . . . .

YOU, LORD, IMMENSE

You, Lord, immense
and chortling friend
fathomless heights,
wide without end

You, Lord, supreme
and robin-breast heart
wooden snare trapped
with you prised apart

You, Lord, full up
louder than pain
Calvary rasp,
sobbing for Cain

You, Lord, outside
and over me tight
heaving your stars
on the pebble-dash night

You, Lord, my end
Nomad King flayed
Begin me again in Wadis of jade